Journey Through The Void (Vol. 1)

Eduardo Reyes

ISBN: 9781073572625

DEDICATION

Thank you to everyone, the events, and creativity that inspired this
collection. This is for creative expression and emotional release.

believe in your dreams, believe in yourself.

ACKNOWLEDGMENTS

Thank you to everyone who resonates with my words.

Inspiration

(A collection of thoughts, ideas, and discovery)

Striving

Striving for the top,

Striving for the most,

Being the best one can be to the best of their ability,

Ambition is one the characteristics of being a leader.

Putting in all the hard work to achieve one's goal,

Appreciate life because not many have the opportunities
that others have.

Unfortunately, some have a disability unable to touch their
goals,

Others are gone but never forgotten.

Always remember never give up,

If you fall get up and try again,

How could you know what you can achieve

if you never try,

Because not trying is worse than quitting.

2
Stay true to you

Stay true to you,

being yourself is the way to go,

Appreciate who and how you are,

Sexual preference doesn't matter,

Those who can't accept it need more maturing.

Originality is better than to copy and paste,

if you're weird or awkward,

Be the person to stand out and not in the crowds,

Do what you love to do without a care in the world.

We all have one life to live, but don't use 'yolo'

as an excuse to do the most absurd,

remind yourself and remember...

Stay true to you.

Society

Society got us all confused,

Used as puppets to the unknown,

What goes on behind closed curtains?

Secrets and conspiracy theories,

not knowing what's the truth and what's a lie,

Trying to figure out what to do to help,

Sitting and feeling conflicted.

People of color are being oppressed,

Screaming for change,

Instead, all we hear are gunshots *bang bang*

Tired of these stereotypical labels,

as if we were canned and separate.

Filed by gender roles and sexuality, when will it all stop?

4
Wall Flower

The wall flower that just stood there

deep within its bubble.

All it wanted was to belong,

To be accepted for its weird shaped petals

and awkward stem,

Its shyness blooming into self-confidence.

5
Weirdo

Seen as the black sheep within the pack

shunned for being different,

wanted nothing to do with the norm

hidden in the dark corner, he/she was the light.

Brightly showing that he/she gave no fucks

dancing to his/her hearts content

ridiculed and made fun of

stepping his/her way down a separate path.

His/her hands formed a gift with words

just one stroke, he/she wrote

"it's okay to be different, be yourself"

his/her words grasping the hearts of many.

A soft and shy voice, generated into a loud roar

echoing throughout the corners of bright light hidden
among darkness.

You

You are worth billions,

Beautiful and smart,

Looking like trillions,

Shit, where do I start?

Self-worth is more important just stick to who you are,

Don't let no one bring you down

From a high pedestal to the ground,

No one should be allowed to do that.

Like the queen that you are,

More valuable than diamonds,

Where have you been at?

Don't you know that you're very important?

One to be cherished and loved,

Wishing I could be the one,

But I'm far from it,

So, I'll continue to make you see,

That you're worth more than you think,

To me you could be everything.

.

7

City by the Sea

Born and Raised,

In the city of palm trees,

early morning traffic,

from Long Beach boulevard to Ocean Avenue.

The city of underground art,

murals and graffiti,

each person with a story,

Cambodia Town and MLK avenue,

A melting pot of diversity.

Striving for peace but war seems to be raging,

respect for all ethnicities,

we are no different from each other.

This city has taught us many lessons,

we should collectively act as one,

from me to you,

A Long Beach Native.

0

Oxygen and a helping hand

Humans are a very complicated and confusing species,

one moment we feel happy and full of joy,

the next we feel empty.

As if a void opened within the chest depriving us of
emotional security,

much like having everything in life but needing what
money can't buy,

this thing that causes warmth within us,

described as a breathless experience,

but causes our oxygen level to rise,

the gift of love and compassion.

It can come in many ways, shape or form

a hug from a friend,

a love letter from the person you've adored for years but
didn't say anything

cause you were scared that they would take your breath
away leaving you numb,

just as it is received, it should be given

show compassion by helping someone in need,

show love to those deprived of oxygen.

9

Networking the downfall

the digital age has us trapped and uplifted, at the same time.

it helps us connect with family and friends, network with
major businesses

But, on the other end of the spectrum

the digital age has us confined like a sheep to its cage.

Too blind to notice the door is unhinged

But, mesmerizing social media has us distracted

restraining the free mind, unable to think for ones-self

looking around dumbfounded.

there's only one way to escape this ice-cold box,

put down that hand-held device

shut off that computer, open your mind.

there's more than just the latest statuses

go for a hike, enjoy nature

walk on the beach, enjoy the air

more freedom, less restrain.

10
The Vulnerable Self

A true form of nakedness

Where insecurity and doubt meet

Face to face

With emotional damage.

These crossroads are the comfort

For being uncomfortable

Peel back each setback

Eat at the core

Being comfortable with yourself

Loving yourself fully.

11
Believe in Yourself

Mind is racing

Mind is clear and calm

Like a switch

I feel more up

After feeling depressed

Months prior.

Before my last year of school began,

my mom was stabbed.

Then, I lost my job.

Focus in School, go to internship

Facing Financial hardship.

Know that you aren't alone,

Through connection

A support system will create Itself.

BELIEVE IN YOURSELF.

Trees

Trees are life,

Trees breathe fresh air

Inhaling carbon-intoxicated Waste.

Starting out as a seed

Sprouting into all shapes and sizes,

Branching out providing

Some shade.

Being chopped and Mowed down,

Reducing clean air supply.

Transplant or re-transplant

Regrown from dry roots.

.

Migration Reunification

Government sanctioned Family separations

Mistreated and locked up

In cages.

Disease, death-written camps

Filled with Asylum seekers,

People plagued by violence.

A new wave of dreamers.

Family Reunification, humane treatment

Unlock and tear down these cages

Release them from their shackles.

Destroy these concentration camps.

.

Thoughts

Thoughts can be influenced

By people,

structured thinking

Decision making mixed

With feelings.

Influencers motivate paths followed

Don't forget you're your own leader

Circumstances can force a change

But there's always action and consequences

If you feel poisoned

Drain the well

Wishing doesn't cut it

Refill your cup

With help and all well

Journey Through The Void (Vol 1)

In health

Heal from the pain

Growth in mindset.

.

What it means to be a superhero

We're all superheroes in training

And always will be

Because one never stops learning

That's not all though

We hold a code of ethics

Don't over step, but remember to Set boundaries.

Conduct yourself professionally,

Start where those in need of

Service are at

The list goes on...

Many situations arise

Trying not to burn

Ourselves out

Brave faces

Empathy or Sympathy

we're all human

Agree to disagree

Fairness over equality

Because in all fairness

We need our title protection.

Crows

The crow,

Jet black in color Iridescent glow

They are self-leaders.

If one of their own are attacked

Crows memorize the face

Swarming on the target

But, if helped

The crow dances

Or sympathizes

Taking away the blues

Of the memorized face of a newfound friend.

When one dies

Mourning takes place

With bowed heads

5 minutes later

Vanishing without a sound

Crows are

Self-less, Respecting

Honoring and Grievers

Of their fallen

Heroes in the shadow

Unless provoked otherwise.

17

Gentrification (a reflection)

The reflection of gentrification

Is an apocalyptic nightmare

A new era

Where hood is replaced

With business.

Displacing families on a

Rent rocket and

It's only going higher,

A better view for those who

Can afford it

Blind to the true cost.

What's the price for living

If I can't afford to live

(Pun intended)

Paying my way to get by

Soon it'll be out of reach.

Knowledge

Knowledge is key

It's true

You can't turn the handle without

Learning how

Now pull.

One door way leading to

Another, then another

Throughout this journey

One learns from others.

Growing, maturing

Innovator, Leader, Creator

Take a stand.

Walk with others

But, don't let others

Walk over you.

Relationships and Friendships

(Feelings of Love, a collection of 'heartbreak', and past events)

Fireworks

Loving you was like the fireworks on fourth of July,

Small explosions of exciting memories

one by one slowly disappearing,

the aroma of gun powder was all I smelled when I was
around you.

Then, you shot the bullet

going straight through my heart,

a misleading illusion

healing took time,

But forgiving you felt like eternity.

Once I crossed that bridge

all that was left was to burn it,

Burn it away with our memories and those small sparks

traveling through this road alone,

I am finally happy.

20

The Gaze

An unfamiliar face stared deep inside me

almost as if she was searching deep into my past

wondering if we had met before

perhaps it was a couple months back, perhaps it was in a
second life.

a bond that was once strongly connected, lost in the
footprints of time

love was rooted deep in our DNA

slowly misconfigured by generations of heartbreak

now I stare back at a blank face, wondering...

He stares back at me, I wonder where we have met before

perhaps it was a few months back, perhaps it was in a
second life

it felt as if we were close to one another, yet so distant

was it love? was it heartbreak?

as I stared deeply, gazing into his past

staring blanking I wondered…

did he think the same?

Our first dance

A protective warmth around our hearts,

growing and learning every step of the way

it was our bridge connecting mind and soul

breathing at the same pace,

heartbeat dancing to the same rhythm.

this dance felt like our first and last,

one wrong step in our routine made us stumble,

gaining momentum again, but the song changed

it became moodier, less uplifting.

as the song reached its end, the sound became tragic

although we held each other's hearts

it became our own time bomb,

self-destruction slowly crept in.

with a hole replacing our beautiful dance floor

our love became two left feet

Journey Through The Void (Vol 1)

our love lost its musicality.

Worth

You are worth billions,

Beautiful and smart,

Looking like trillions,

Shit, where do I start?

Self-worth is more important just stick to who you are,

Don't let no one bring you down

From a high pedestal to the ground,

No one should be allowed to do that.

Like the queen that you are,

More valuable than diamonds,

Where have you been at?

Don't you know that you're very important?

One to be cherished and loved,

Wishing I could be the one,

But I'm far from it,

So, I'll continue to make you see,

That you're worth more than you think,

To me you could be everything.

Ghost Lover

She was in love,

but this love was forbidden,

she chased it knowing the risk.

Together they created a false reality,

deeper and deeper she fell,

losing herself in the process.

The love was exposed and now she feels heartless,

he soon married.

Burying what remained of the love-struck girl.

She became a ghost,

roaming inside of her own casket,

searching for her old self,

searching for flesh to call her own.

24

String of Love

They say love is blind,

Which is why some of us wear glasses,

Get the reference?

Let me explain how caring for someone too much can be
dangerous,

It starts off with a loose rope filled lots of laughs,

Tied together so tight by the forming friendship, it starts to
become a noose,

Not one you wish to have around your neck,

But, a bracelet you just can't rid of.

Caring so much as to not damage the bracelet in anyway,

Holding on dearly to the person who forged it in the first
place,

Then one day it begins to ware itself out.

Arguments and space, drifting each other away unable to

Journey Through The Void (Vol 1)

refill those gaps,

Finally, you have had enough and the bracelet you once
held dear rips itself away from the wrist,

The wrist that once cared too much,

For something that eventually became...

Nothing.

The Way

The way you make me feel is like the first leaf dropping on
the first day of autumn,

the sign of starting fresh and anew,

my insides feel like a cup of warm abuelita chocolate,

turning into butterflies when you talk to me.

my heart begins to beat and skip along the side walk,

wearing a coat with glowing and warm hand-made stitches,

I devour every one of your thoughts, ideas, and simple
details you speak to me of

like chocolate chip cookies.

traveling to my stomach but the information and familiar
taste files into my brain,

you are a loose leaf and I am the breeze carrying you along,

as I hold you close I will shield you from the rainy days,

I am the chocolate glaze to your bread and together,

we make a donut.

A letter to the one I love

I have gone through trial and error just to find you,

my eyes have poured endless rivers,

my heart has "shattered" repeatedly.

Rebuilding itself from the hairline cracks of temporary
misleading's,

I hope that you can accept my flaws and insecurities,

because when you go through many wars there is bound to
be repercussion.

when I seem to be over protective of you,

it is because I have lost myself, time and time again,

when I say, "I love you", know that I mean it,

although those words have been the death of me,

I will use them to give you life.

27

Phoenix

Our love used to feel like a blossoming rose,
Summer is coming but are petals just wilted,
Cutting our roots out of jealousy,
anger and guilt for things I couldn't control.

Everything happened so fast
like a ball to the face,
I'm left with anger and pain,
As I sit here thinking how it all went wrong.

someone else has your attention,
that "friend" knew his intentions,
hating this position, I'm in
stuck between a wall and a sea of flames.

get over it and move on,
or let this situation burn me,
picking myself up from the ashes of our memories,

burned and bruised but like a phoenix,

I will be reborn and take flight.

Wilted Petals

By Eduardo Reyes

Where have you gone? I thought you'd stay for long,
I'm waiting at the bus stop, its cold out
I packed up my belongings and took off.

We used to stay up all night and lip lock,
in dark silence, I forget your name now,
where have you gone? I thought you'd stay for long.

I remember your touch, warm and soft
feeling butterflies, they fly out my mouth
I packed up my belongings and took off.

All I see is a silhouette of us
a beautiful watered flower in drought,

Journey Through The Void (Vol 1)

Where have you gone? I thought you'd stay for long.

Wilted petals slowly but surely ready to drop

our memories sinking into the ground

I packed up my belongings and took off.

listening to the sound of our downfall

I appreciate the dead silence sound,

Where have you gone? I thought you'd stay for long

I packed up my belongings and took off.

.

Letter to my future something

I want you to know that I am flawed,

Built up then broken down,

Rebuilding myself,

It's been a journey of solitude,

Know that I love open communication and honesty,

If there's something you don't like please talk to me,

As I shall do the same.

I'd be myself around you all the time,

I'm weird and stupid funny,

Not funny but my stupid jokes might make you laugh,

I'm not about the drama but if there's ever a problem,

I hope we compromise.

When I give my all,

I hope you don't take advantage,

Journey Through The Void (Vol 1)

Of my time, attention, and affection

If I come off a little too strong,

Let me know.

Penguins

I know you love penguins,

you love penguins so much

I saw the spark in your eyes,

When I bought that shirt with Slippery Pete.

you said I looked cute in it

so, I wore it on occasional dates,

even bought you a stuffed penguin

you named it Mr. cuddles.

I thought of myself as the penguin and you were my
glacier,

perhaps it was the heat of miscommunication

or the distance between our voices that caused us to drift

the gap became too wide,

I tried to hold it together.

the "I love you's" began to sound faint

self-centered and oblivious, huh?

Journey Through The Void (Vol 1)

forcing me to jump into the freezing ocean with clipped
fins

eventually we floated our separate ways, and I'm still
drowning.

Curves

Everyone loves curves,

the one most attractive is the one your lips make.

There are days when that smile is accompanied by tears,

days when that smile curves into grief and silence.

Everyone deserves to smile without a care

happiness that does not diminish when it rains.

Like a rainbow after the storm

I wish to see that endless array of light.

If darkness ever comes over you

I shall offer you my personal rainbow to see you smile.

Affection

Love is

unshaken and unbothered,

I'd lie if I said a piece

Of me wasn't in love with you.

Loneliness is

Missing a piece of you,

You didn't know was missing

Affectionless.

33

The Ending of Relationships

Ending a relationship

A goodbye

Maybe temporary

Or the

Ending of terms

Every circumstance is different

Yet, it feels the same.

Kind of like growing

A second heart and

Ripping it out

After each term.

Dream to Illusion (Letting Go)

The heart feels heavy when hurt

A hole punched through

Where happiness resided,

A dream turned illusion.

Tears run down,

Missing you

Instances and moments

replaying over and over

Then, it hurts.

I thought we were on the same page

Yet, you skipped to the end of our story

Maybe its temporary

Or maybe I did care too much

And it might've been too much.

Although you're here

Journey Through The Void (Vol 1)

you left without warning

I guess there's never a right time

For bad news.

Hurt and confused

I still think of you,

What do I do?

Leave it be and move on?

It's hard to let go.

At First Sight

Love at first sight

How would I know it's there?

Lately it's been about swiping left, swiping right

Where's the connection?

Lost in the disconnect

Of the internet

And dating apps

Feeling like love

At first sight

Is out of sight

Blinded

I cannot see what love

Looks like

Forgetting the feeling

A world without butterflies

So, when they ask

"What does love at first sight look like"

Tell them you're waiting until

The next migration

The return of butterflies.

Lust

Lust is passion filled, yes

A box of sweet nothings

Although every morsel

Tastes like heaven

It's only temporary.

Beautiful Brown Eyed Girl

Beautiful brown eyed girl,

Sun kissed glow

Radiating from

Sunlight.

You're like the sun

So, I won't get close

Burned away by your Stare,

I stand at a distance

Admiring you from afar.

Time

Time is precious

So, don't waste it

An investment with an interest

Of intimacy and togetherness

As the pages turn

The other person rips Themselves out

a page break

A blank space trying to figure

Out what happened

Left with a tear

And a sturdy spine

A chapter book

Missing your pages

Inserting fresh blanks

Journey Through The Void (Vol 1)

Rewriting a story lost

To time.

Communication

Conversation, a communication

Of words and energy

An exchange of glances

And smiles

Mix in some laughter

Opening the doors to relationships

A mutual friendship

Building bridges

As the two or multiple

Walk across feelings

And emotions transfer

To one another

May it last long

Some bridges burn

Enjoy the ashes

Journey Through The Void (Vol 1)

Beautiful Memories

blown in the wind.

4U

Love VS Trust

As 21 savage says,

"You can love someone

And still stab them in the back".

rather you trust

Than to love

Remember trust is earned

Not given

Same as respect.

Anyone can love you

But, not everyone will Respect or trust you.

Be aware though

Don't sleep on your surroundings

Even those who are close can turn

Snake.

41

Heart Break

Heartbreak feels like ripping
Your heart from the chest
Trying to figure out what went wrong.

Heartbreak teaches lessons
Some more painful than others
Trust broken, emotionally hurt.

Time mends the scar
Invest in yourself to heal the pain
Love yourself to the fullest
Believe in yourself.

Crushes

Crushes, just as the name implies

I like you but I'm afraid to say

In fear of my flame dousing out

Then, my logs of courage

Being stepped on

Which is why I crush on you

To protect myself

Although I might give hints

Might not, you'll never know.

Attention

I'm an attention seeker hoping that I catch yours,

Did I come on too strong?

I want to get to know you

Take a second, ask a

Few questions

Turn the minutes into hours

Deconstructing your walls.

Building trust and communication,

Love may feel like a far feeling

I know you've received it from all the wrong places

But it isn't out of reach

Smile beautifully

The sky is clearing.

44

Affection (Pt.2)

Affection

I feel that I am too affectionate

Are we a moment or will we last?

I hope you cherish my kisses

Small lipped, yet I promise

I ain't bad.

Memorize every touch and caress

A brown body that may get

Attached

To your affection

I just don't want to get

To close because

When you get too close to the sun,

it burns.

The Void

(A collection of fear, depression, and loneliness)

45

The Ruins

As I walk along these cold gray walls

the air feels chilled, filled with vast empty space

I turn left, at the end of the hall there is worry.

My younger siblings, financial issues, identity theft. All in
one room.

I close the door but on most nights, it swings open.

I turn around and walk the other way

Down this hall, there is confusion and sadness

questioning life and my choices, wanting friends around,
but I'm alone.

Caught between feeling sad and what feels like episodic
depression

perhaps I just complain too much, the reality of growing up

I slam the door, but on most nights, it swings open.

Down the main hall, the atmosphere is different

the walls are colored, the air is warm and fuzzy

there is happiness, accomplishments, and the value of life

I try to remain here, but I am unstable as the pillars.

46

The Dark Days

On some days, I shine as bright as the sun,

Talkative and embracive,

On some days I feel like shit,

Mind racing and wanting to cry.

"You can change the way you feel",

but my mind sometimes doesn't register,

My emotions pay my mind to change,

But sometimes my mind doesn't register.

48

Strange Figure

a pair of tired eyes gazing into my past

struggle, pain, and happy memories

lessons learned, with goals achieved.

love found, love lost, love destroyed

eviction, being homeless, asking for money

starving stomach,

how does this person know so much about me?

exposing my wishes and desires

taking note of the toll I paid going through each booth,

as I was cuffed and put into foster care,

forced to mature with mental scars peeling my old being
away.

slowly suturing a new personality into the body of my
adolescent self

moved back home to an estranged relationship,

repaired through therapy and counseling

one parent still homeless, but slowly it began to pull itself
together.

with all its beautiful cracks and missing pieces

this mirrored image stared back at me, trying to separate
fantasy from reality.

Human Touch (Alone)

Human touch is needed by everyone,

Babies and mothers' chest to chest.

Newly dating couples fluttered with emotions,

holding pinkies for the first time.

Safety, security, and relief of tension.

For an instant, we're able to breathe

Without the worry of feeling alone.

My Journey (an overview)

Let me take you all back to a simpler time,

I used to live with my mom and sisters

Two-bedroom apartment, cozy life

The manager kept the rent money and

Eviction knocked hard with a 9mm.

I was not at home when the eviction

Happened, But I felt the blows from my mom's

Anger. Grandma swooped in to save the day,

Only to file a restraining order on my mom.

Pomona bred the start of my new life.

My sisters and I came back to Long Beach.

The relationship with my estranged father,

Exploded with tears and anger.

The next Day, I returned with my mother.

Things went Down from there, staying in motels.

Or in my grandpa's musty smelling van with small

Blankets. One cold night, I go to my dad's

House, asking if I could stay the night. With

Nowhere to go, He says he needs to call the

Caseworker. Shockingly, Cops are called.

In the back of the car, I am headed

To L.A. The next day, I'm in Montclair.

I am taken to a caseworker who

Buys me the essentials and sends me off

To Fontana, Now I'm in foster care.

Living here was not tough but I had tough

Times. I was made fun of and punk'd on, But

I stuck to school as an escape from all

The sudden changes to my life. I left

A year and a half later to my dad.

Therapy healed the open wounds between

My father and I, not so estranged but

More like a brotherly relationship.

I graduated high school on honor roll,

Now, I'm a social work graduate.

Walking in the dark,

Through trial and error I am learning

More about myself as I balance me

Life between school, work, and family life.

Thank you.

Loneliness

Wanting to be loved,

Ridding oneself of their loneliness

A hole in the heart,

a silent consumer Eating away at the thoughts

Of wanting to be in the arms

Of another,

Their warmth filling the hole

Feeling not so alone.

52

Lost

What's it like to feel lost?

It feels like being trapped

Within a maze

Sometimes the turns

Lead down a long path.

Sometimes dead ends are met

Filled with confusion

Watching the days go by

Losing concept of time

Turning to walk the other way

Glued to the wall

Pondering an escape

I'm let go, free to walk

Wondering my maze,

I continue to walk.

Anxiety

I walk outside,

There's a tornado coming towards me

I try watering my grass

But somethings different.

It's half yellow, half green

Proud of where I am

Half way rotting

Frantically, I try watering the yellow patch.

Sad to say,

the tornado is slowly catching up

Hoping I end up in the eye of the storm

Where it's calm and at peace.

Irrational Fears

I have them...

But they come out as jokes

*for example, *

The elevator is going up,

Jams,

Stops

Now I'm waiting for this toaster oven to drop.

One of my fears,

I die by gunshot

It might be my surroundings

Where the unexpected can happen

Wrong place, wrong time Paranoia.

Angels in the outfield

"It could happen"

Pessimistic thinking

Journey Through The Void (Vol 1)

You're breathing and alive

You might think it's exaggerated thinking

Although life is good

My mind continues lurking.

Trapped

Trapped within myself

Looking for an escape

But, darkness surrounds me.

I try to run

Clutched in its grasp

With a depressed grip

I shake free

Flooded by light

I walk tall

Smile and cheery

Yet, the darkness looms over me.

E-Shutdown

How have you been?

You don't look so good.

See I've been standing tall

Without the water works.

Not able to feel

Because my pipes

Are rusted,

they must've dried up

When I closed them off.

58

Lost Souls (Meth Dance)

Cook it, shoot it

The rush is endless

All it takes is one try.

It's like dancing with the devil...

Everyone's situation is different

But, the results are the same

They become

A lost soul with two left feet,

Walking backwards,

The dance never seems to end.

A crowd gathers

Yelling "you need help, please stop"

Except these curtains never close.

Hypnotized from its grasp

The crowd is trapped, forced to watch

Journey Through The Void (Vol 1)

Entertainment turn into a horror show.

The performer is now a former shell

Of themselves, unrecognizable at times.

Dancing with the devil, all it takes is one try

Stepping with two left feet, walking backwards

Remember what it was like to dance

Alone, and walk forward?

The only way out for the performer is

To break their own foot

Acting on their own accord,

The crowd can empathize and encourage

Sometimes falling on deaf ears

Sometimes the curtain drops.

THANK YOU FOR JOURNEYING THROUGH
THE VOID (V.1)

Support by informing friends or family about the importance of vulnerability and mental health.

Volume 2

Coming Soon!

Journey Through The Void (Vol 1)

Made in the USA
Middletown, DE
26 June 2020

10164486R00056